PORTFOLIO 3

METROPOLITAN SEMINARS IN ART

Portfolio 3 · *Expressionism*

by John Canaday

ART EDITOR AND CRITIC
THE NEW YORK TIMES

THE METROPOLITAN MUSEUM OF ART

EXPRESSIONISM

The Painter and the World He Creates

OUR first portfolio centered around the idea that a painting is first of all an experience. In our second we looked at the world as interpreted in a series of paintings within the immensely broad field of realism. Each realistic painter was content with the natural appearance of things as the starting point for interpretation.

But even so, none of these painters merely copied the appearance of things. Some, like Harnett, Velazquez, and Chardin (Plates 13, 19, and 20 in Portfolio 2), modified nature so subtly that at first glance their intention seemed only imitative. Others, like Van Eyck (Plate 10 in Portfolio 1 and Plate 16 in Portfolio 2), seemed downright photographic in detail but were not at all so in total effect. And we saw in every case that the expressive element of the paintings came from the painter's modification of natural appearances rather than from his ability to reproduce exactly the world around him.

Since this is so it would seem reasonable that the less a painter is obliged to stick to the natural look of things the greater his expressive range should be. This does not necessarily follow, but some painters have applied the principle, and this portfolio is concerned with paintings where the modification of visual reality is so great that it reaches the point of distortion. We will see why the painters in question thought it necessary to depart so violently from the "real" look of things.

Our subject is expressionism, and the paint-

ings we are going to see will be more intense and on the whole more personal than the ones we have seen so far. Every great painter has an individual style, but the expressionist painter's work is likely to be more sharply individualized than the realist's, more dramatically his own, sometimes to the point of eccentricity. This individuality is quite natural when a painter is more interested in probing his own soul than in reflecting the world of ideas, more interested in explaining a moody or tempestuous inner world than in revealing a basic harmony in the one around us.

No matter how much the realistic painter modifies nature we can still conceive of the painted objects existing in the real world. He changes them somewhat, and he puts them into an order that gives them meaning, but they are still real. But the expressionist paints images so very exaggerated or so distorted that he takes us away from the familiar world into one of emotion and feeling—at least, that is his intention. In extremes the expression may even become hysterical or nightmarish. The very personal nature of expressionism may keep the observer from entering the artist's world because the artist may speak in terms perfectly clear to himself but puzzling to others.

As a working definition of expressionism then: expressionism in painting is the distortion of form and color for emotional interpretation. If we want to establish as neat as possible a dividing line between realism and expressionism, we can add to this definition

Figure 1

The Starry Night:
Free Expression and
Studied Expression

When we first see *The Starry Night* it appears to have gushed forth onto the canvas of its own volition. The whole picture swirls with a fierce, surging energy far removed from our ordinary associations with a starry night. In one corner the moon is as fiery as a sun (*Figure 1*), and the sky is filled with stars that seem to be whirling and bursting from the force of their own inner light. Through the center of this explosive sky there winds a form we cannot identify as a cloud or as the track of a comet or even as the Milky Way, which it is supposed to be. In such a sky such a form really needs no explanation as a natural one. It is an expressive one, an invented one, far removed from the physical truth of whatever form may have inspired it.

The curling, rushing movement of this galaxy across the picture is repeated in an upward direction by the cypresses springing from the foreground as if they were tearing themselves free of the earth. Back of these trees the fields and hills of the countryside surge and swell around the only quiet objects in the composition, a steepled church and some small houses, their windows yellow with light.

The Starry Night is so highly charged with emotional fervor that it is tempting to think of its having been created through some kind of spontaneous combustion. Our knowledge of Van Gogh's life—his emotional torment, his unsuccessful search for peace with this world, his terrible loneliness—all this, as well as our knowledge that he was subject to periods of irrationality, seems at first consistent with his producing such a fervid picture in an inspired frenzy or even in an almost hypnotic state.

The fact that we feel such immediacy in *The Starry Night* is a tribute to Van Gogh's genius for emotional expression. Our enjoyment of the picture comes in large part from our feeling

that the distortion goes beyond the point where we can accept the possibility of objects existing as the painter has represented them.

According to a dictionary definition, expressionism involves the "free" expression of emotions. We have been pointing out that all the forms in great painting are organized into compositions that are far from free if free means spontaneous and uncalculated. So when we say that expressionist painting is a "free" expression, we must still remember that what may look like a very free painting may still be a highly calculated one. A perfect example is *The Starry Night* (Plate 25) by Vincent van Gogh. *The Starry Night*, painted in 1889, is established as a classic of modern art.

of direct emotional communication with the painter. Although the picture is a personal revelation, it speaks in terms perfectly clear to the observer also. Van Gogh's paintings always seem to have come fresh from the easel; we seem to be in the painter's presence—even after we discover that this is a calculated picture, not a spontaneous production.

And very thoroughly calculated it is. For one thing there is the way the upward twisting of the cypress forms is used as a counterforce, a kind of brake, to the forward rush of the comet-like form across the sky. Both forms benefit by the contrast since neither one is allowed to overpower the rest of the picture, as either would have done without the balancing influence of the other. The most dramatic dark in the picture—again, the cypresses—is played in another balance against the most dramatic light—the fiery moon—on the opposite side of the picture. (Imagine the difference if either the moon or the cypresses were shifted into the center.) Among secondary elements the church steeple helps unify the composition, first by echoing the form of the cypresses and also by interrupting the insistent line of the hills against the sky. The rushing line of the horizon might otherwise carry us too swiftly to the edge of the picture and out of it. This steeple-and-hills relationship is a restatement of the cypress-comet relationship, a repetition of the main theme, and is a major reason why a picture of such violent force is complete and self-contained instead of chaotic. And all the other elements in the picture, including the direction of each brush stroke, are caught up in the flow of movement determined by these major forms.

All the organization of the picture, its balance, contrast, echo, and rhythmic flow, was of course perfectly conscious on the part of the artist. He probably painted the picture rapidly. It is so vividly direct that it is hard to believe that he reworked any part of it, but the composition is so skillful that we could not believe it was accidental or "inspired" even if we had no evidence to the contrary. But we do have this evidence. We have Van Gogh's preliminary drawings for various parts of the picture and at least one earlier study of the same subject, as well as his letters over a period of many months with references to his plans for developing it.

In his letters Van Gogh talks again and again about his plans for pictures, describing his progress toward the expression he wants. He once wrote a friend who had admired the intensity of feeling in one of his pictures of some gardens, ". . . that was not accidental. I drew them many times and there was no feeling in them. After I had done the ones that were so stiff, came the others. . . . How does it happen that I can express something like that? Because it has taken form in my mind before I start on it. What I am doing is not by accident but because of real intention and purpose."

As for his color, which is so right and seems so pure that we feel he had nothing to do but reach for paint ready at hand, he tells elsewhere in his letters of the trouble he had in determining exactly the kind of black (greenish, or bluish, in relation to the surrounding colors) for painting cypresses. And although he frequently used certain colors straight out of the tube, for maximum intensity, he did so only after long experiments in color relationships that were no less complicated for having ended in the desired effect of extreme directness.

And so Van Gogh, like all great artists, was a theorist and craftsman as well as an emotional human being. But this theorist also describes himself as working in a "dumb fury" at times and once, after painting all day without even stopping to eat, he wrote, "I shall do another picture this very night, and I shall bring it off."

There is nothing really contradictory in this combination of feverish creation and the application of theoretical principles. Expressionist art like Van Gogh's, by the nature of its intensity and its extremely personal quality, reaches its pitch of achievement at times when the artist is so "inspired" (for want of a better word) that his whole accumulation of knowledge and technical skill is at his command for immediate, as if spontaneous, use. But to think of an artist "inspired" to create a picture without preliminary spadework is as unreasonable as to imagine an actor giving an inspired performance without having learned his lines or a poet creating a masterpiece in a language he does not know. *The Starry Night* is an inspired painting if ever there was one, but its creation was possible only because Van Gogh worked toward it for so long. (He wrote, "I wonder when I'll get my starry sky done, a picture that haunts me always.") The painting is so consummate an expression that even Van Gogh's other completed paintings are, in effect, preliminary studies for it. Its creation must have been for him the most exalted and ecstatic emotional release.

Van Gogh and Our Time

In our other portfolios we have insisted that painting is an expression of its time. How does *The Starry Night* accord with this idea? We could say that in its extreme individuality it would not have been painted in a time other than our own, when individual freedom is a basic concept in our thinking. We could also say that in the need this lonely painter felt to communicate with his fellow man through painting, his art reflects the isolation of the individual that is a frequent corollary of his freedom. We could skate on very thin ice and suggest that in its violence, its agitation, its excitement, *The Starry Night* is a reflection of our age. All these arguments are at least partially true; it is certainly true that stylistically (in its design, in its manner of paint application) it is impossible to imagine *The Starry Night* belonging to any other time. But conceptually, as a personal expression, it is not much more of our time than of any other time—perhaps for the very reason that its creator was never able to become really a part of the life around him, as he so desired.

Expressionism in an Old Master

Expressionism is a new term used particularly in connection with modern art, but the principle of distortion of form and color for emotional expression appears in the art of some of the old masters too. El Greco's *Christ at Gethsemane* (Plate 26), painted just three centuries before *The Starry Night*, is every bit as expressionist as the modern painting and even makes its effect through similar distortions.

As far as subject matter is concerned El Greco is obliged to conform to the letter of the Bible story, but he treats it in an individual (and expressionist) manner. Christ prays on the mount, his eyes lifted toward the apparition of an angel. Rocks, robes, clouds, and diaphanous shafts and veils of light intermingle until, in spots, one cannot be distinguished from another. The most curious element in the picture is the cavelike or miragelike form beneath the figure of the angel that encloses the sleeping disciples (*Figure 2*). They are shown in odd, unnatural attitudes, not suggesting the relaxed quality of sleep at all but rather an enchanted or magically transfixed state that removes them as witnesses of the divine events in progress nearby. At the extreme right, within a mystically luminous landscape, we see Judas approaching with the Roman soldiers (*Figure 3*).

Compositionally *Gethsemane* and *The Starry Night* employ surprisingly similar devices. The various forms in both pictures are tied together by swirling, eddying rhythms continuing without interruption between landscape and sky, uniting earth and heaven in ecstatic harmony. Both pictures are painted in vivid colors. In both, the rhythmic flow of line is picked out in supernatural lights. The distortion in the cypress trees is even similar to that of the robed figure of Christ. Both forms are elongated into conelike shapes, swirling and twisting in the intensity of their upward striving.

The composition of El Greco's *Gethsemane*

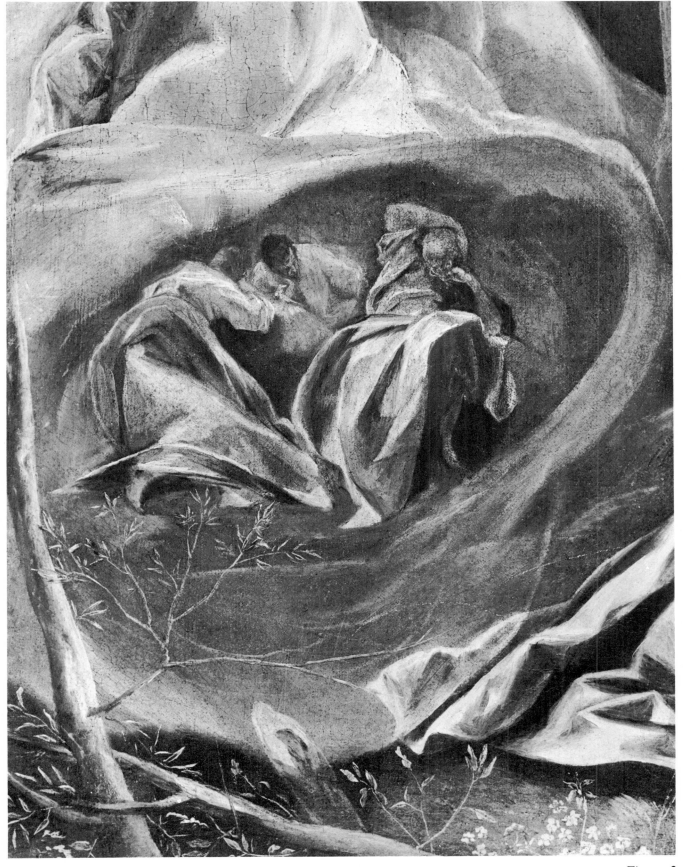

Figure 2

Figure 3

is more complicated than that of *The Starry Night*, but the main flow of line that knits it together can be traced around the strange form enclosing the sleeping disciples, on up along the edge of the peaked boulder—the very summit of the mount, and then into the clouds that fill the upper right part of the picture. This sinuous line is very like the line of the Milky Way in the Van Gogh, although it is less obvious.

Behind all these surface similarities, however, the two pictures are different in conception. Van Gogh's is a personal vision of overwhelming force. El Greco's intensity is somehow thinner, stretched to the breaking point. The El Greco has elegance—it makes its appeal in more sophisticated terms than the Van Gogh. Its mystical quality is the result of a colder and subtler calculation, for all its staggering brilliance. The El Greco is a sumptuous painting, and although it is a religious one, its first appeal is through its sumptuousness, its elegance, its finesse, and even its sensuousness. These comments are neither derogatory nor irreverent. The great art of El Greco makes sense in these terms as Van Gogh's would not.

El Greco is so individual a painter that the appreciation of his art has had a curious history as tastes have changed and as ideas of what painting should be have shifted back and forth. In his own time, for that matter, one of his paintings was rejected by Philip II of Spain, who had commissioned it for an altar in the Escorial. The Church recognized the mystical power of El Greco's style and under its patronage he steadily increased the element of distortion in his painting, apparently to everybody's satisfaction.

Succeeding generations, however, lost the understanding of El Greco's art until, not too long ago, he was either ignored or, at best, relegated to a minor place in art history as an interesting eccentric. His distortion was even explained as being the result of astigmatism! You will still hear this absurdity from time to time. If it is necessary to refute it, we can point out that astigmatic vision would not produce these distortions in the first place, and anyway El Greco painted numerous pictures, particularly portraits, in which the degree of distortion is slight. In *The Burial of the Count of Orgaz* (Plate 27) he combines his more realistic style with his expressionistic one in the two parts of the same picture.

The lower half shows the Count's body being placed in its tomb by Saint Stephen and Saint Augustine in the presence of surrounding relatives, friends, and dignitaries. There is a certain amount of elongation in the drawing of these thin-faced, melancholy aristocrats (*Figure 4*), but on the whole the figures in the lower half can be conceived of as existing in the form in which El Greco painted them.

In the upper half, however, we see first an angel who holds the soul of the Count in the conventional form of a naked babe, represented here as more shimmery and gauzelike than fleshly (*Figure 5*). The angel is more distorted than the human figures below it, and as we go on up toward the figure of Christ on his throne the distortion becomes greater and greater. Saint John the Baptist, shown kneeling, is a fantastically elongated figure with a tiny head and odd swellings and contractions in the arms, legs, chest, and waist.

These distortions are repeated in the other celestial figures who surround the saint as he intercedes with Christ for the newly arrived little soul. The scene takes place upon various levels made up of the same luminous unidentifiable forms that twist through the *Geth-*

Photo by Anderson

Figure 4

Photo by MAS

Figure 5

semane. In short, El Greco has brilliantly combined a realistic earthly scene and a visionary heavenly one, modifying his manner appropriately from realistic to expressionistic.

El Greco and Van Gogh

We do not know a great deal about El Greco as a person. He may or may not have been of a particularly mystical or visionary temperament. In any case, he developed a highly individual style and was successful with it. The style was emotionally expressive, it is true, but we do not feel, as we cannot help feeling in the case of Van Gogh, that personal emotionalism becomes so fused with technical procedure that they become identical. El Greco apparently developed his style objectively, calculating its effectiveness and making the most of it as a professional artist rather than an emotional human being. With Van Gogh expressionism was a personal release; with El Greco it was an intellectual achievement.

Expressionism and Moral Statement

The three expressionistic paintings we have seen so far are all visionary pictures, but the range of expressionism is wide. Our next illustration is at the opposite pole and brings us back to contemporary painting. Rouault's *Two Nudes* (Plate 28) deals with brutal truth instead of rapturous hallucination, with degraded worldliness instead of elevated spirituality. It is the kind of picture that makes people say, "With so much that is beautiful, why paint something so ugly?" Not only the subject—two hideously naked prostitutes—but also the very look of the picture seems ugly to most people. The color, instead of being decoratively "beautiful," seems turgid, the drawing coarse and heavy-handed.

Yet this is a painting by a man who on occasion draws with the most delicate precision, who has painted conventionally beautiful and

Figure 6

reverent interpretations of mystical religious subjects, whose color frequently has the clear brilliance of stained glass. Why did he paint this "ugly" picture? If the man is a mystic how can he choose this subject? If he is a great draughtsman why does he draw like this?

Actually, there is no paradox here: *Two Nudes* is noble in conception and its drawing is consistent with its message.

Two Nudes is an outraged cry of protest against man's inhumanity to man, against corruption, meanness, and human degradation. In social and humanitarian terms it is a thoroughly moral picture. The painting is a condemnation, an accusation against a world that can be so brutalizing and degrading. It is secondarily a condemnation in general of the animalism of lust.

Now, these ideas are impossible to present in a picture of conventional prettiness. Rouault slashes at his drawing in coarse, heavy lines expressive at once of his own anger and the brutishness of the women (*Figure 6*). He distorts the bodies into heavy, lumpy forms that are indeed ugly, as bodies. The color is scrubby, roughly applied, suggestive of fresh tints turned morbid, as if affected by the evil the painter reveals. And the answer to the question "Why paint this instead of something beautiful?" is that the whole world in any of its aspects is the painter's province. What he most deeply feels, he must paint, in the most appropriately expressive way.

But, of course, *Two Nudes* is a beautiful picture. Technically it is beautiful in the absolute control of drawing. For all the appearance of coarseness and license, the thick boundaries of the forms are perfectly controlled to describe these forms, and to describe them with appropriate emphasis. Even the distortions are beautiful in their powerful, expressive quality. They could not have been created by an artist who had not passed through apprenticeship in the kind of accurate, detailed drawing that looks more difficult. Finally, above all, the subject is not base or vulgar. It

is noble, if faith in man's goodness is noble. The subject is not presented lasciviously. (Could vice be made more unattractive?) Nor is it presented in cynical acceptance of evil. It is presented as a protest, and to protest against evil is to recognize the possibility of good. In all Rouault's work there is a fundamental faith in man's redemption through his recognition of evil and his rejection of evil.

It is in this implication that *Two Nudes* finds its meaning. We are shown ugliness in terms of such violence that we must recognize it—and reject it.

From any other point of view *Two Nudes* is only a powerful and repellent image of two grotesquely ugly, dehumanized creatures.

The City: Marin

From our discussion so far it appears that expressionism must always be associated with the morbid, the tragic, or the visionary. To a large extent this is true. "Distortion for emotional expression" suggests violence and intensity, although the whole emotional range, including feelings of peace and quiet joy, can be expressed by appropriate distortions of form (into simple, quiet shapes) and appropriate color (subdued, soothingly harmonious ones). In practice, however, these quieter emotions are expressed by poetic realism. Expressionism is given the field when subjects are intense rather than serene, agitated rather than peaceful. But for a painting using expressionistic devices to interpret a scene more cheerful and familiar than most, we can look at John Marin's water color, *The Singer Building* (Plate 29).

A photograph of this subject or a realistic painting of it would be reduced to the rigid parallel vertical lines of the skyscrapers, with their flat walls regularly punctured in a rigid pattern by windows, and to the horizontal lines of the shopfronts, the sidewalks, and other forms at street level. There would be very few forms at off-angles, and these forms would be small and inconspicuous. Even the crowded traffic of automobiles and people would be frozen in place, clotted into masses not suggesting their turmoil of movement. Rigid horizontal and vertical lines suggest quietness, orderliness, permanence. They are the standard framework for a picture of static character.

Now, this is the opposite of the impression a city makes, of course. The city is busy, pushing, noisy, excited, crowded, confused. The city is dynamic. And this dynamic character is immediately relayed to us by Marin's painting. If we try, we can decipher in the lower part of the picture some shapes suggestive of the elevated, of streets, shops, and the rest. But the important thing is that the sharp, strong angularities that interrupt one another, breaking and shifting to other angles, are all suggestive of action and excitement, whereas a photograph is of necessity static in effect (*Figure 7*). Much of the fascination of modern photography is that it can freeze action. But to freeze action is the opposite of expressing it, as Marin wants to do. And in the end, this expressionist approach is a "real-er" statement of what a city is than the photograph would be. Yet some of the most expressive parts of the painting are not recognizable as objects. In the lower half many of the sharp, emphatic lines are simply that— lines, not parts of buildings or other objects. And just above center-right the wavering oval of pinkish color represents nothing at all but serves as an expressive transition from the activity of the lower half of the painting to the relative quiet of the upper half.

This transition is the most important but least conspicuous achievement in the picture. The action and excitement takes place at street level. We are embroiled in it, but as we go up in the picture the excitement grows less, the forms are less interrupted, there is less contrast of dark and light, the colors are more delicately washed in, until finally the peaks of the skyscrapers escape into the open sky. Furthermore, if you examine the color you will see that its upper and lower parts are dominated by different groups of colors. Reds and oranges

are called "hot" colors and are psychologically associated with action and excitement. Blues and greens are "cool" and associated with quietness. Marin makes the transition from the strong, exciting colors to the quiet ones in several steps—including, for instance, a change in the color he quite arbitrarily uses for the window openings in the buildings. This color transition goes hand in hand with the transition from the active, broken shapes and angles in the lower half to the quieter shapes in the upper half. Leonardo da Vinci used the same

Figure 7

warm-to-cool color progression in the landscape background for the *Mona Lisa* (Plate 6, Portfolio 1), going from golden browns to silvery blues, although the yellowing of centuries of varnish has obscured the original contrast, making the cool passages much warmer than Leonardo intended.

Finally, we must remind ourselves that like any good picture, *The Singer Building* is an organization of line, shape, and color into a composition. The angular lines that express the excitement and confusion of the city also tie the composition together by repeating, buttressing, and echoing one another. Again we see that objective skill and technical control are the means to an expression (not a description) of a subject so agitated that objectivity and control might at first seem out of place. Realizing this, Marin makes a point of retaining an effect of great spontaneity. He is a first-rate water-color technician and carries the medium far beyond the delicate (and too often washed-out) tones usually associated with it. Some of his color is applied from a full, wet brush. In other places you will be able to see the grainy quality of the rough paper where he has dragged a nearly dry brush across it. These contrasting textures are an important element in the variety and excitement of the picture.

The City: Kirchner

The Singer Building plunges us into the city and surrounds us with its stimulating sound and movement. It is essentially a cheerful, vigorous interpretation, full of the booming optimism and sense of youthful power and flourishing growth that we like to think of as typically American. It was painted in 1921 when the American boom was under way and the chastening depression years had not become part of our national experience. A feeling of unlimited vitality filling the air of American cities during those years of fabulous growth is directly expressed in Marin's painting. At almost exactly the same time (1922) a German

expressionist, Kirchner, shows us a contrasting idea of "city" in *Two Ladies in the Street* (Plate 30). (Notes on German expressionism are included under Kirchner's name at the end of this portfolio.)

A German city of 1922 was a very different place from New York. Germany was only four years away from its defeat in the First World War. The terrible period of shock and dislocation was producing some of the worst social deformities in the history of our civilization. *Two Ladies in the Street* is full of morbid introspection, of melancholy brooding, of the soul-sickness of a defeated and groping nation. There is a haunted quality in the figures of the two women. Their fashionable clothes have been turned into witchlike silhouettes, and although they are part of a crowd, we feel first of all their isolation in some private and unhappy world of disturbing preoccupations. The picture's colors are totally unreal, from the olive green of the skin to the brilliant red, blue, and yellow of the background. The angular treatment of the blue and black area may somewhat suggest the angularities of Marin's city and may carry some of the same suggestion of noise and activity, but it is a faint echo in a picture that relays to us first of all a feeling of unnatural stillness. The face of the central figure regards us uncomprehendingly, or suspiciously at best. She stands in an odd, half-crouched, retreating attitude. The strange little taxi behind her and the figures making up the crowd on the other side of the picture are as wooden and doll-like as toys, increasing the effect of unreality. It shows a world without meaning, yet somehow threatening, full of ominous foreboding—exactly the opposite of the booming enthusiasm of Marin's city.

The City: A Child's Vision

It is worth taking a moment here to comment parenthetically on yet a third expressionistic painting of a city—this time by a nine-year-old child who, as far as he was concerned, was

Figure 8

simply painting a city the way it looked to him (*Figure 8*). An understanding of the art of children has grown in recent years as a corollary to the development of expressionist theory in modern painting. Whereas children used to be trained to curb their natural exuberant expressiveness in painting, to "be neat," and to "keep the color inside the lines," and, in short, to defeat every spontaneous release of their natural bent for putting ideas into pictorial form, they are now encouraged to paint exactly as they please on the principle (quite sound) that they are unable to apply rule and theory in picturemaking but may have a natural response to psychological values of colors, lines, and shapes. The nine-year-old who painted the picture of a city is no Marin nor is the eleven-year-old who painted the one of a hurricane (*Figure 9*) any Van Gogh, but the resemblances

of these spontaneously invented forms to those in *The Singer Building* and *The Starry Night* is more than coincidental. The children have made extremely direct translations of their feelings into images that seem right to them. The adults have done the same thing, but not so innocently; their translations are conscious translations and must involve formal knowledge and theory, since the feelings they are describing involve corresponding maturity, depth, and complexity.

It is easy to overrate children's painting as artistic endeavor, which, of course, it essentially is not, and to credit many a lucky accident as an expressive intention. But at the same time it is good that we have learned that expression must often be released through forms and colors that are not accurate transcriptions of nature and that we have learned to under-

16

Figure 9

stand the nature of painting done by children as well as the art of expressionism on this basis.

Expressive Convention

Once we have come to understand the expressionist idea, many paintings that cannot properly be called expressionist begin to mean more because their distortion takes on for us a new significance. Simone Martini's *The Annunciation* (Plate 31), painted in the Italian city of Siena in 1333, is a good example.

The picture cannot mean much if we expect it to make its statement in realistic terms. The beauty of the color and the opulence of the elaborately ornamented gold ground would appeal to us in a sheerly visual way, but that is about all. Many average gallery visitors, in fact, look at such a picture with the assump-

tion that its unrealities are the result of limitations in the painter. He didn't make the faces "natural," they think, because he was unable to; the Virgin's position is "funny" because he was incapable of drawing her in a natural one.

Now, the Annunciation has been painted hundreds of times and in hundreds of different ways, including extremely realistic ones. Whether or not Simone could have painted this one more realistically than he did is beside the point. He painted the figures in his *Annunciation* with their odd, even outlandish, features, with their elegant distortions, and in the particular attitudes and particular combinations of lines that we see because that was the way he wanted them to look and that was the way his patrons wanted them to look. Naturalism, or realism—whichever you want to call an imitation of the way things look—

17

Figure 10

simply was not the goal. Any assumption that an artist's first job is to imitate reality to the very best of his ability can blind us to the expressive virtues of pictures like Simone's *Annunciation.*

A great deal of the "distortion" here is nothing more than a convention, familiar and popular at the time, a formula intended to express an extreme spiritual delicacy and purity (Plate 32). Sienese painters adopted a pale, blond, slender, small-headed, long-faced physical type that looks odd and even unattractive to the newcomer to Sienese painting. Every age adopts its own set of exaggerations or variations of female beauty. You have only to look at a few magazine covers of "glamour girls"

to see some exaggerations that will look laughable or outrageous in a few years—not to mention a few centuries. And six centuries separate us from the Sienese ideal type.

These hyperrefined, even neurasthenic types, so removed from all the robust flesh that was so tempting and so subject to temptation, were established expressions of the medieval Christian virtues of chastity and preoccupation with things spiritual. At the same time it was also a type of considerable sophisticated appeal in more worldly terms. Our knowledge of the life of those times shows us that renunciation of the flesh was more popular as an ideal to be celebrated than as a way of life to be practiced. There was a great overlapping of the idea of

18

spiritual refinement and the idea of fashionable fastidiousness. It is not at all unlikely that fashionable beauties of the day did their best to approximate this painted ideal, just as women today somehow manage to modify their faces and figures to correspond with whatever "new look" is being imposed upon them at the moment.

So we must accept a large element of fashion even in Simone's *Annunciation*. In the hands of a second-rate painter this element could have dominated the painting and reduced it to doll-like affectation. But in the hands of a master like Simone, this nervous, artificial delicacy can be extremely expressive once we have accepted the distortions involved.

The Angel Gabriel has just alighted before the Virgin, interrupting her at her devotions. His elaborate cape, as suggestive of fashionable luxury as of heavenly splendor, still flutters about him. There is nothing natural about the beautifully designed swirling lines of this cape any more than there is anything natural about the swirling Milky Way in Van Gogh's *Starry Night*. But as an expression of graceful alighting movement it could hardly be bettered.

And in the figure of the Virgin we are a step closer to our definition of expressionism—distortion for emotional interpretation. As she receives the message—written in raised letters issuing from the Angel's mouth across the surface of the picture (*Figure 10*)—the Virgin recoils in a combination of dismay and reverent acceptance. The artist has designed the figure in a curiously angular and broken way suggesting the shock of the announcement in terms, almost, of physical impact. Compositionally this angularity contrasts so effectively with the grace of the alighting Angel that both figures benefit from it.

Three Crucifixions: Rubens

We could argue that for an Annunciation or any other mystical subject an unrealistic treatment is the only appropriate one. But to see

whether this is necessarily true we can compare three treatments of a single subject, the Crucifixion.

The first of these, *Christ on the Cross* (Plate 33) by Rubens, was painted in the seventeenth century by a master who was under no technical limitations whatsoever. The laws of perspective and anatomy had been discovered and codified long since. For Rubens their use was second nature. He had at his fingertips the whole range of knowledge for the creation of effects of light and shade, the various ways of giving illusions of depth, of making forms look round and solid. If you recall our comments on baroque painting in Portfolio 2 (illustrated by another Rubens, his *Prometheus*, Plate 18), you will understand why Rubens paints the scene as realistically as he does. He appeals to the emotions through our own physical experience with sensations of pain or pleasure. Is this Crucifixion really an interpretative picture at all? Rubens gives us a magnificently painted male nude who is Christ only by association of ideas. There is little or nothing to supply the mystical connotations of the subject; we ourselves supply them by foreknowledge. As far as the painter's contribution is concerned, there is nothing inherently divine in this figure of a man nailed to a cross. It is not irreverent to say that if we didn't already know otherwise, this might easily be some Olympic champion undergoing torture or, more accurately, a well-muscled actor caught at a climactic moment of a fine performance. And the whole production is wonderfully staged. The lighting, the backdrop with its illusion of storm and distance are marvelously dramatic. And they are so real! They almost make us feel we are there. And that, of course, is the whole intention.

Now there is virtually no distortion at all in the Rubens. The features are twisted in agony, the muscles of the arms and chest are strained tight—but none of this is a distortion of nature. It is, on the other hand, a kind of extreme naturalism under given physical circumstances.

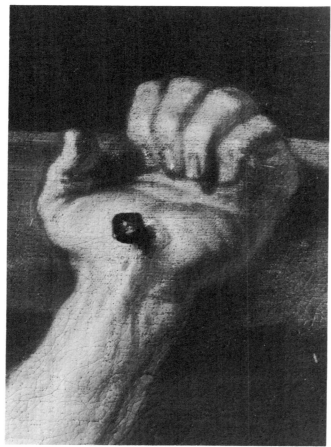

Photo by Foto t'Felt

Figure 11

Not only is there no distortion, there is hardly, even, any exaggeration. Everything in the picture is represented at its highest dramatic pitch, but there is nothing in it that could not have been reproduced directly from nature. The picture still makes its effect today in very much the same terms as it did when it was painted almost three and a half centuries ago.

Three Crucifixions: El Greco

Now, returning to El Greco, the great expressionist among the old masters, we find that he is not content to let us supply the mystical and miraculous spirit of the picture while he serves as stage manager. He wants to make mystery and miracle inherent in his version of the Crucifixion, *Christ on the Cross with Landscape* (Plate 34); to do so he must depart from real appearances. He creates as background an otherworldly space shot through

with ambiguous forms and supernatural lights such as never existed on earth. We can easily imagine the human being who posed for Rubens's Christ—in fact, we don't have to imagine him, we see him. But if we had to imagine El Greco's Christ as an existing human being, he would be a grotesque one. But we are not tempted to imagine him so nor does it bother us that the figure does not actually hang from or seem actually nailed to the cross, as Rubens's does (*Figure 11*). Rather, the figure in the El Greco seems magically suspended, as if weightless (*Figure 12*). Everything is unreal or half real. If we did not already know the story of the Crucifixion we would still be aware that the subject of this haunting picture was no ordinary scene of torture but a divine event.

Three Crucifixions: Master of the Saint Francis Legend

Whether the Rubens or the El Greco is the better picture is not a question. Some people will be more moved or more interested by one, some people by the other, some people equally but in different ways by both, and some people may prefer to either of them the *Painted Cross* (Plate 35) by an unknown master of the Middle Ages.

The figure on the cross certainly looked much more real to the people it was painted for than it does to us. But they did not demand, or even conceive of, realistic painting as we know it. The painter has made some effort to round out portions of the figure in a naturalistic manner, and this effort is fairly successful in the smaller figures. But even so, realism in the terms we have been discussing was beyond his conception also. The loin cloth remains primarily a decorative pattern of line (*Figure 13*), the hair is so highly conventionalized that it is out of the question to think that the painter tried for anything like realism, and the ear is snuggled in between the hair and the beard like an afterthought (*Figure 14*). And

20

there is no effort at realistic relationship of the various figures involved. There are four scales, descending in the order of the figures' importance. The largest, of course, is reserved for Christ alone; the Virgin and Saint John share the next largest; the two mourning angels at the ends of the arms of the cross are a degree smaller; and finally the mere human being, kneeling at Christ's feet, is appropriately accorded the minimum size. Thus any worldly reality is immediately denied. From the beginning the figures are expressive symbols, not realistic representations. And the figure of Christ, which would be merely inept conceived of as a realistic image, takes on a deeply moving spiritual reality. Probably this painter was being as "real" as he knew how. But he has had to depend for the most part on variations and rearrangements of certain conventional approaches shared by the other painter-craftsmen of his day. Perhaps he would have been completely naturalistic if he could have been. But need we worry about that? Does it really make any difference? His intention was

to achieve an expression of the mystery of the Crucifixion, and he achieved it, by whatever means. The "distortions," whatever their origin, determine the character of the painting, and through them it speaks to us.

Expressionism and Allegory

The more we see of painting the more we realize that there is no one way of relaying a message. For different men, at different times, the message is expressed in such different forms. We will conclude our discussion by showing how a modern American artist and a medieval artist centuries earlier chose different ways of giving us similar messages.

Before 1500 there appeared in France a certain Shepherd's Calendar, called *Le grant kalendrier et compost des Bergiers*. Like others of its kind it was an almanac combining popular misinformation, accepted superstitions, astral diagrams, medical hints, horoscopes, and pious comments on virtue, vice, heaven, hell, and the culture of the soul. It was an

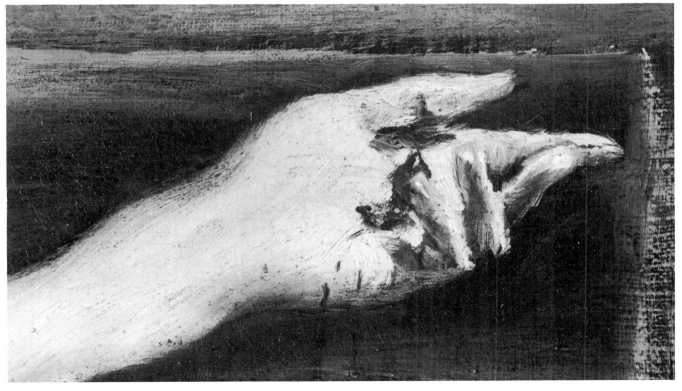

Figure 12

everyman's version of the intricate compendium of medieval learning and was illustrated with woodcuts, of which we reproduce one (*Figure 15*). The picture is an allegory accompanied by an explanation which translates to this effect:

Mortal man living in the world is like a ship on the sea or a perilous river carrying rich merchandise which, if he can reach the desired port, will make him happy and rich. The ship from the moment of setting out clear to the end of the voyage is in great peril of being sunk or captured by enemies. Because there are always perils at sea. Thus is the body of man living in the world; the cargo which he carries is his soul, the virtues, and good works. The port is Paradise where all who arrive are wonderfully rich. The sea is the world, full of vice and sin.

(*Homme mortel vivant au monde est comparé a navire sur mer ou riviere perilleuse portant riche marchandise, lequel s'il peut venir au port que le marchant desire, il sera heureux et riche. La*

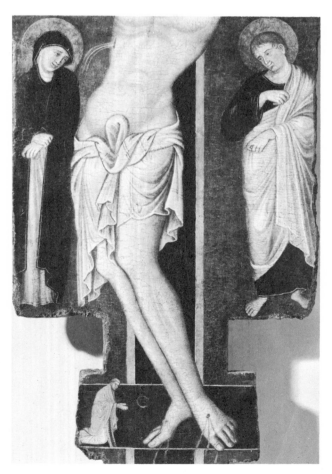

Figure 13

navire quant entre en mer jusques a fin de son voyage est en grant peril d'estre noyee ou prinse des ennemys. Car en mer sont tousjours perilz. Tel est le corps de l'homme vivant au monde; la marchandise qu'il porte est son ame, les vertus et les bonnes oeuvres. Le port est paradis auquel qui y parvient est souveraynement riche. La mer est le monde plain de vices et pechez.)

The illustration of this allegory is an engaging combination of explicit realistic detail and symbolic conventionalizations in the service of spiritual statement. The ship, the captain, the mast with its sail, and the anchor are drawn without consistent relationship as to scale. The water is represented by conventionalized lines perfectly acceptable to the medieval eye as a stormy sea, and both God and the devil are shown as literally as the man himself. Nothing in the picture is modified for expressive purposes. It is an allegorical diagram that must be "interpreted" in a sense as literal as its accompanying explanation must be interpreted from one language to another for a foreign reader.

This approach, of course, is the opposite of expressionism, where no form is allegorical or realistic, where every form carries its message within itself by means of shapes and colors invented by the painter. In Ryder's *Moonlight Marine* (Plate 36) the tossing sea is not meant as a symbol of the dangers of life in the world; even less is the frail ship meant to suggest man's body charged with the cargo of his soul, protecting it from the perilous waters of evil. Yet in its emotional effect the picture is close to the lesson of the medieval woodcut.

Ryder was a great romantic painter whose art can be called expressionistic in pictures like this one where the forms have been reduced to a few silhouettes calculated to convey to us the thought and feeling of the painter without dependence on detail or literary associations. There is nothing here but a vast sea, a vast sky, a moon, the unreal shapes of some clouds, and a small boat nearly obscured. "The artist should fear to become the slave of detail. He should strive to express his thought

Figure 14

Figure 15

and not the surface of it," Ryder said. Van Gogh could have said the same thing, but the forms in *Moonlight Marine* are different from those in Van Gogh's *The Starry Night* because each of the painters finds his own expression through forms personal to himself. "No two visions are alike," Ryder said, "and those who reach the heights have all toiled up the steep mountains by a different route. To each has been revealed a different panorama."

This is true of all great painting, but it is most pointedly true of expressionism because each artist tells us in such direct, personal, and intimate terms of the panorama revealed to him. We share Van Gogh's vision of cosmic force swirling through the night; El Greco's elegant refinement of mystical passion; Rouault's horror of man's evil and his conviction of man's goodness; Marin's exultation in the city's clashing energies. And with Ryder we understand (because through his painting we feel) his sense of man's journey through the world, where he may be so small in the infinite scheme, so threatened by its elements, but for a while so secure as he keeps his boat on course over the water, beneath the clouds, by the light of the moon.

Although the paintings we have been seeing in this portfolio on expressionism modify the appearance of nature, sometimes drastically, they do not depart so far from the actual appearance of things as to leave them unrecognizable. An exception can be found in some areas of Marin's *Singer Building*, where it is difficult or even impossible to identify the pattern of jagged, crossing, conflicting lines with the specific objects that must have inspired them. In this painting Marin is at once an expressionist and an abstractionist. Abstract painting, the most puzzling (and sometimes the most infuriating) aspect of modern art, is the subject of our next portfolio. We will see that abstraction, like expressionism, is an important element in the art of the old masters just as it is the all important one in the art of certain contemporary painters.

Notes on the Painters

Vincent van Gogh, 1853-1890, Dutch

25. THE STARRY NIGHT, 1889

Oil on canvas. Height 29". The Museum of Modern Art, New York, Lillie P. Bliss Bequest

Van Gogh has been the subject of so much romanticizing that it is customary now to think of him as a mad genius. He was a painter of exceptional originality who toward the end of his life was subject to periods of irrationality. Diagnosing his case in retrospect, some doctors believe his ailment was of an epileptoid nature. But he was sane. A lunatic might have painted with Van Gogh's intensity but could never have painted with his control.

The circumstances of Van Gogh's life are well known. Born in Holland into a family with a conventional background, he was unable to lead a conventional life because he developed an extreme sense of isolation. He was a short and ugly man, hypersensitive, with no talent for social intercourse, although he yearned for friends and companions. Various unhappy love affairs increased his sensitivity, his awkwardness, and his shyness, but did not decrease his passion to give his love to fellow human beings.

For a while he studied for the ministry, but there too his intensity defeated him. He could not conform, and after a heartbreaking experience among poverty-stricken miners and peasants in Belgium he abandoned this career to devote himself to painting.

The story of his relationship with his brother Theo is one of the most touching to be found in any documented life. Vincent's letters to Theo are a living record of his hopes, ambitions, and despairs, as well as illuminating notations on his methods of work. Theo's to Vincent show why this brother was the artist's chief emotional (as well as financial) support throughout an agonized life. The letters are available in several compilations and are more revealing than any biographies of the man.

Van Gogh committed suicide not during one of his mental attacks but in a period of depression, unwilling to continue a life which he thought was becoming a burden to others. He died having sold almost no paintings. For an artist the sale of a painting is gratifying quite aside from the money involved because it indicates in the most direct way that his effort at expression and communication does have meaning and purpose. This gratification was denied Van Gogh. He says in his letters that he is certain his work will one day be recognized, but he could hardly have foreseen its current popularity. Exhibitions of his paintings have set all-time records for attendance at one-man shows. He is so generally admired that reproductions of his paintings are offered as premiums in sales promotion campaigns.

The immense popularity of Van Gogh's art is not connected with a general recognition of its tragic implication. Rather, the public is attracted by its vigor and its ornamental brilliance. On the other hand, the student of Van Gogh is likely to exaggerate the tragic implication of his art in the light of the man's tragic life. The implication is there, but if Van Gogh is a great artist it is because his art at its best rises above his personal tragedy to achieve a vision of such force as *The Starry Night*, rather than sinking below it into the despondency that occasionally appears in his earliest work.

El Greco (Domenicos Theotocopoulos), 1541-1614, Spanish

26. CHRIST AT GETHSEMANE, 1590-98

   Oil on canvas. Height 40¼". The Toledo Museum of Art, Toledo, Ohio

27. THE BURIAL OF THE COUNT OF ORGAZ, 1586

   Oil on canvas. Height 15' 11⅞". The Church of Saint Thomas, Toledo, Spain

34. CHRIST ON THE CROSS WITH LANDSCAPE, ABOUT 1610

   Oil on canvas. Height 6' 2". The Cleveland Museum of Art, gift of Hanna Fund

El Greco, "the Greek," is the name that was adopted for Domenicos Theotocopoulos, who was born on the island of Crete. He studied in Italy, perhaps under Titian, although his style has more in common with that of a younger Venetian painter, Tintoretto. About 1575 El Greco went to Spain where he spent the rest of his life, for the greater part in the city of Toledo.

El Greco's career is full of curious twists. He is thought of as the painter who has most fully expressed the mystical intensity of Spain, yet he was foreign to the country by birth, by training, and, so far as we know, even by temperament. In spite of his success during his lifetime his reputation waned thereafter until he came to be regarded as a provincial artist with an eccentric style interesting for its novelty but inferior for the same reason. For a while he was all but written out of the history of art; it was not until the beginning of this century that his work was properly re-evaluated.

It is hard to say which is greater, El Greco's influence on modern expressionism or modern expressionism's revelation of El Greco's quality. And it is just as difficult to say in which direction his art is more rewarding, as the direct emotional experience he intended it to be or as the intellectual one we find in realizing the calculation and objectivity with which he went about creating this emotionalization. The effectiveness of the formula he worked out is demonstrated by the response it creates in the layman, who accepts the most violent of El Greco's distortions without question but is puzzled or moved to wrath by distortions no more extreme in contemporary work.

El Greco is the only one of the old masters who is better represented in America than in Europe, with the natural exception of Spain, because he was less avidly collected than comparable masters during the eighteenth century so that his work was available when Americans began to collect.

El Greco was never averse to repeating a successful picture, and, worse, his compositions were frequently taken over in toto for a second execution by his studio followers. Furthermore, these repetitions make him a conspicuous target for the contemporary forger. For these reasons there are quantities of inferior or false El Grecos, where his dramatic quality becomes merely theatrical, his distortions merely grotesque, and his emotional intensity nothing but a kind of nervous wriggling. Of all painters, El Greco most clearly shows how precarious and how indefinable is the line between the legitimate use of a consciously developed manner and its prostitution.

Georges Rouault, 1871-1958, French

28. TWO NUDES, ABOUT 1905

   Oil on paper. Height 39¼". The Metropolitan Museum of Art

Rouault was one of the fauves, who have been mentioned in the Notes at the end of Portfolio 2 in connection with another member of the group, Raoul Dufy. Rouault alone among the fauve artists is preoccupied with subjects of social consciousness and religious mysticism. The other fauves continue the tradition of urbanity, ornamental gaiety, and fashionable nuance that is a steady tributary to the stream of French painting. This "boudoir painting," as it is called by those not sympathetic to its refinements, dominated French art in the eighteenth century, finding its most poetic statement in the work of Watteau, its most callously professional one in that of Boucher, and its most vivacious one in that of Fragonard. In the nineteenth century Renoir draws heavily on the tradition in his sensibility to young women, and in the twentieth Matisse and Dufy reflect the fashionable indulgences of the Riviera in much the same spirit as their eighteenth-century progenitors reflected the life of the court and the demimonde.

Although a fauve by association and by certain technical characteristics, Rouault is much less related to the painters we have been mentioning than to men like Rembrandt and Daumier, who have been concerned with man's spirit in conflict with the world's potential for degradation.

Rouault is deeply affected by Catholic mysticism. In his later style the harsh outlines apparent in our illustration become filled with glowing blocks of color, resembling pieces of stained glass held within their black lead boundaries. The resemblance is no coincidence. Rouault worked for a time at the repair of medieval cathedral windows. His Catholicism is sympathetic to this art form, which was the medium for some of the most impressive statements of Christian mysticism during the age of faith.

Rouault is also one of the most powerful lithographers among modern artists. Lithographs (drawings on stones prepared in such a way that the drawing may be printed many times from the stone onto paper) may be printed in color, as many of Rouault's are, but his black and whites are of exceptional richness and force.

What we have said here is typical of Rouault at his best. As is true of any artist, Rouault's work should not be accepted blindly picture by picture as typifying his maximum achievement. It is a small heresy to say so, but it is nevertheless true that many of Rouault's paintings suggest formula. Some of them, beneath a veneer of importance, have only the decorative lightness of so many other fauvist pictures, without their grace. But every artist, as has been said elsewhere in this text, deserves to be judged by his best work, and in his best work Rouault is a great painter in his generation.

John Marin, 1870-1953, American

29. THE SINGER BUILDING, 1921

Water color on paper. Height 26½". The Philadelphia Museum of Art

Marin occasionally painted in oil, but he is first of all a water-colorist. He used the medium with unusual force. To some people, "water color" carries a suggestion of the wishy-washy, a relic of the days when its practice was considered appropriate for genteel ladies because it was the least messy and the simplest of painting techniques. Actually the manipulation of water color is extremely demanding. Its range is wider than the usual timorous and uninventive water-colorists indicate. Marin used water color with more strength than most people find in other mediums.

The usual characteristics of water color are not characteristic of a Marin. Instead of capitalizing only on pale tints (one advantage of the medium is that it permits their use without loss of brilliance) Marin uses the full range of intensity, including black. Water color permits infinitely subtle gradations from color to color or value to value, but Marin seldom uses these "graded washes," painting instead in blocks and strokes of solid color or strong gradations. Water color is usually applied very wet; Marin frequently applies it so dry that it has something like the quality of chalk or crayon. You will find Marins which deny each of these generalizations, since he explored water color in all its capacities, but he found his most personal expressions in the least conventional use of the medium. The influence of his work has been so great, however, that these "unconventional" uses of water color are becoming its new conventions. (These comments are enlarged in a later portfolio devoted to technical processes.)

Marin, an American, incorporated into his work various features of European "isms" without identifying himself directly with any European school. We have called his *Singer Building* expressionistic, and so it is, but not in the sense that he is a follower of the German expressionists or the French fauves. The broken angularities in the lower part of the picture (even more marked in some of his other pictures) suggest cubism and must stem from it, but Marin is not applying cubist theory. It is always difficult to explain why one painter can draw from several sources, as Marin seems to have done, and produce an original art, whereas another painter may draw from the same sources and yet produce only a shallow pastiche, imitative superficialities. Whatever the explanation, Marin remains his own man.

He is also particularly American among contemporary painters. His work is full of the vigor and excitement of America's great cities, but in another aspect, his paintings of the Maine shore, he reveals an equal sensitivity to the strength and excitement of natural forms.

Ernst Ludwig Kirchner, 1880-1938, German

30. TWO LADIES IN THE STREET, 1922

Color woodcut. Height 27¾". The Museum of Modern Art, New York

A year before his death Kirchner said, "My goal was always to express emotion and experience with large and simple forms and clear colors." This is a good definition of the goal of German expressionism in general and not a bad one of fauvism, the French form of expressionism developing at the same time. It is an elastic definition in that the temperament, the emotion, and the experience of the individual painter will determine the variations he makes of the "large and simple forms and clear colors."

In the case of the Germans, who especially have come to be designated among modern painters as expressionists, these forms tended to be rigid, ponderous, and coarse. The adjectives are not meant to be unflattering, any more than the opposite adjectives—fluid, graceful, and refined—are meant to be flattering to the French fauves. Such forms were the means the Germans adopted for powerful expression. Their proper use demands as much skill, and as subtle skill, as does the proper use of forms we are more accustomed to thinking of as "artistic" ones. They are appropriate to the dark and melancholy areas of the spirit explored by Kirchner and his fellow painters.

These fellow painters are specifically Karl Schmidt-Rottluff (1884-   ) and Erich Heckel (1883-   ), who with Kirchner called themselves *Die Brücke*, The Bridge. Their association dates from 1905 in Dresden, giving us a date and birthplace for the German expressionist movement. They were soon joined by other painters who had already been affected by the same spirit in the air that animated Die Brücke.

Fauvism, expressionism, and cubism, three art movements experiencing something like a triple birth, were all influenced by primitive art. Kirchner's *Two Ladies in the Street* may look not only primitive but brutal to those accustomed to thinking of slick technique as a prerequisite of pictorial art. But the aim of Die Brücke was to revitalize art, and like the fauves and the cubists in France, they discovered in the art of primitive peoples the vitality they felt had gradually drained away from European painting.

Die Brücke, it is important to remember, had no idea of "going primitive." They did not seek the absurd and impossible goal of a return to primitive innocence. But since they did learn from primitive art the lesson of broad, direct forms, it was inevitable that the look of primitive art should be reflected in this new hypercivilized one. The faces of the women in our illustration are suggestive of African tribal masks for that reason. At least they are superficially so. Actually Kirchner has transmuted these primitive forms into new ones that are not only not expressive of primitive vigor but are on the opposite hand the nightmarish reflection of a moribund civilization.

As a postscript to this very brief statement on German expressionism, we should add that in 1912 a second group, calling itself the *Blaue Reiter* (Blue Rider), was formed by Wassily Kandinsky and Franz Marc. Kandinsky's art is considered in our next portfolio, Abstraction; after a period of exaggerated popularity the work of Franz Marc, composed largely of repetitious designs of red or blue horses and deer, is seldom seen. Paul Klee, also a member of the Blaue Reiter group, developed away from expressionism in a personal direction. He too is discussed in a later portfolio. Emil Nolde's name should be mentioned as an important one in Die Brücke, as should Max Beckmann's, since he is one of the most forceful painters stemming from it. Käthe Kollwitz and George Grosz may also be called expressionists, although their art is concerned with social protest and satire rather than with the more personal explorations thought of as typifying the movement.

Simone Martini, about 1283-1344, Italian

31. THE ANNUNCIATION, 1333

   Oil on wood. Height 8′ 8″. The Uffizi Gallery, Florence

32. Head of the Virgin from THE ANNUNCIATION

Simone painted his great *Annunciation* in 1333 for the altar of the chapel of Sant'Ansano in the Cathedral of Siena. In this cathedral, one of the most elaborately elegant structures in the world, Simone's *Annunciation* was certainly in its perfect setting. The picture is as exquisitely turned, as richly aristocratic, as decorative as that building, and like it, it is only secondarily a spiritual expression. It is first of all an ornament of the rarest beauty, achieved by superb technique in the service of taste cultivated to the verge of overrefinement.

Simone painted at a time when Italian artists in other cities were excited over the new realism. In the first decade of the century the painter Giotto had covered the walls of the Arena Chapel in Padua with a series of frescoes phenomenally realistic beyond anything any living person had ever seen. Giotto's innovations were so fundamental that they changed the whole direction of painting. It is not even too much to say that Giotto set the direction of painting for the next six hundred years, that is, until our own century.

The other great innovators between Giotto's century and ours built on his reference to nature, conceiving as he did that the "real" look of things was the foundation of pictorial art. It was not until the twentieth century that painters broke away from Giotto's idea that painting necessarily refers to the world of visual reality no matter how the painter may modify it.

In the midst of the excitement created by Giotto's revolution the Sienese painters alone preferred their own highly developed style to the new one. Only a few painters tried to graft the two styles. The nearby rival city of Florence became the "boom town" of art while Siena continued to cultivate its stylized tradition. Simone is the last of the purely Sienese painters whose art is not quite affected by the anemia that soon began to enervate Sienese art. Subsequent Sienese painters, especially Sassetta, have left us some entrancing pictures, but even the most enthusiastic admirers of Sienese art have to admit that in contrast with the humanistic vigor of Florentine realism the attenuated Sienese spirit becomes charming rather than meaningful, inventive rather than creative.

A taste for Sienese painting is an acquired one and must be based on the recognition that here is the flowering of a long tradition foreign to our own. Simone's Virgin may be the Queen of Heaven—Siena was a city dedicated to the Virgin—but she is equally a courtly lady and a spiritual symbol. She is part of that aspect of medieval life that produced such affectations as the systems of courtly love and inspired the lyrics of the troubadours, the fash-

Photo by Brogi

ionable world of chivalric jousts, of banquets and entertainments whose descriptions make the galas of international café society today look like peasant festivals.

Historically, Simone has an extracurricular importance as part of an international school of late medieval painting centering in Avignon in France, where he worked between 1339 and 1344. He also had visited the court of King Robert of Anjou at Naples in 1317. He was a friend of the poet Petrarch, whose polished and aristocratic sonnets are a literary parallel to Simone's pictorial manner.

Photo by Foto t'Felt

Peter Paul Rubens, 1577-1640, Flemish

33. CHRIST ON THE CROSS, ABOUT 1610

Oil on canvas. Height 7' 2⅛". Royal Museum of Fine Arts, Antwerp

Rubens, whose *Christ on the Cross* is included in this portfolio, also painted the *Prometheus Bound* of Portfolio 2. The reader may be interested in comparing the two pictures for himself, the subjects being as far apart as a pagan legend and the Christian story, to discover whether Rubens has approached them with any significant difference in his point of view.

The pictures are good for comparison since they are coincidentally pictures of men in agony. There is also a certain parallel in subject, oddly enough. Prometheus brought fire to men and was punished for it in the manner illustrated. Christ brought redemption to men, and his crucifixion, while not a punishment, is the price of that gift since he died to give it. It has been said of Rubens's work that no matter what his subject, every one of his paintings is invested with the air of triumph. This may be the basic unifying factor in the two paintings.

Master of the Saint Francis Legend, XIII century, Italian

35. PAINTED CROSS, ABOUT 1280

Tempera on wood. Height 6' 2". The Philadelphia Museum of Art, Wilstach Collection

The Master of the Saint Francis Legend designates an otherwise anonymous Italian artist who painted Christ on a cross (Plate 35). Such crosses were produced in large numbers during the latter part of the twelfth century and in the thirteenth. (The one illustrated was painted about 1280.) The ones that still exist vary in size and quality according to the size and wealth of the church for which they were originally commissioned.

There is some question as to where these painted crosses were placed in the church. Sometimes, it appears, they were put on the altar, but they may also have been suspended over it from the ceiling, especially in the case of some very large ones. High up within the shadows of the vaults, illuminated by the flickering gleam of the candles below, they must have had the quality of a vision. They may also have hung high on the wall of the apse, the terminating wall of the church behind the altar, or have surmounted the rood screen when one existed.

In any of these locations the cross would climax the architectural scheme of the Romanesque (early medieval) church, with its steady progression of repeated architectural forms down the nave to the altar. In the earliest crosses the figure of Christ is straight and erect, placed symmetrically along the center line of the cross, with the eyes wide open and neither face nor body giving any indication of pain. Writing on the subject Henry Clifford has said, "As time goes on, the head gradually droops, and the body starts to bend slightly to the left, under the weight of suffering. The next development is to show the figure of Christ dead on the cross and the body curved out more and more. While it is not an infallible rule, roughly speaking these painted crosses can be dated almost by the degree of curvature up until the time of Giotto.''

Clifford also describes one of these crosses in the small Italian town of Casape, situated in the Roman Campagna between Tivoli and Palestrina, that was formerly in a small field chapel that the peasants used to pass on their way to work in the vineyards: "During the war of 1914-1918 the women of Casape, believing especially in the power of Christ and Saint John, picked away bits of the paint from these figures with their fingernails to send to their sons at the front. When it was tried, after the war, to remove it to Rome for conservation, the townspeople, jealous of their greatest possession, threatened violence, and the cross now hangs neglected in the local church, a prey to worms who in a few years will reduce it to dust.''

Albert Pinkham Ryder, 1847-1917, American

36. MOONLIGHT MARINE, 1870-90

Oil on wood. Height 11⅜". The Metropolitan Museum of Art

Ryder is the mystical poet of American painting. He was an eccentric and a recluse: "The artist," he said, "cannot be a good fellow."

In many ways Ryder exemplifies a popular conception of the artist as a lonely soul dedicated to his work and wedded to poverty, isolated within his personal world of impractical sensitivities and subject to fits of "inspiration," especially during the later years of his life when he never left his studio before nightfall in the belief that daylight was too strong for his failing eyes. The studio itself was such a litter of ashes, milk bottles, and every kind of trash that it was necessary to clear a path in order to walk through it.

These eccentricities are always recounted, yet they are unimportant in the face of Ryder's zest for life. In his writings at any rate, and he wrote a great deal, he makes constant reference to the joy he takes in his work. "The artist needs but a roof, a crust of bread, and his easel, and all the rest God gives him in abundance." "Exultantly I painted until the sun sank below the horizon, then I raced around the fields like a colt let loose, and literally bellowed for joy." "I am in ecstasies over my Jonah [he was working on a painting of Jonah and the whale]; such a lovely turmoil of boiling water and everything."

Unhappily, the Jonah, like too many of Ryder's paintings, is also a turmoil of darkening and cracking paint. Ryder was not a conscientious craftsman, and his paintings are encrustations of many layers of thick paint of differing consistencies. As every painter should know, if these various layers dry at different speeds they create tensions that finally pull the surface to pieces. Virtually all paintings are ultimately subject to some degree of cracking, but a good craftsman will minimize the danger, while Ryder's carelessness has reduced some of his best work to ruinous condition less than half a century after his death. Fortunately the moody turbulence of his subjects is such that the darkenings are not entirely out of harmony—a small comfort.

Next to painting, Ryder's passions were music and literature. He draws frequently from Shakespeare and Wagner, among others, for subject matter. The adjectives "poetic" or "lyrical" are immediately called to mind by his pictures. He occasionally wrote verse himself. Lines like the following ones suggest the poetry of another mystical painter-poet whose spirit had much in common with Ryder's, William Blake, or another recluse, Emily Dickinson:

Who knows what God knows?
His hand He never shows,
Yet miracles with less are wrought,
Even with a thought.